I0840961

THE LOCAL BODY

E.J. Kemper III

TABLE OF CONTENTS

Dedication

I dedicate this book to Mount Pilgrim Baptist Church, the church that God has graced me to lead. You are a great people. And a testament to the greatness of our God. My continued prayer is Lord bless Your people!

Copyright © 2019 by EJ Kemper III

FIRST EDITION

FOREWORD

EJ Kemper III gives a fresh look into the local church. He masterfully uses the **seven systems** in the **anatomy** of the human body, God's crowning work of creation, as the **Seven Systems** of the local body of Christ, the church. Because of the teaching found in **"The Local Body-A Picture of the Church"** we have clearer insight into the functions and roles of the church as an **Organized Organism** that is an **interrelated** and **interdependent network** of ministries. Each system functioning specifically but yet interdependent and related to each other under the command of the **Head, Jesus Christ**.

This book will help to inspire each member to appreciate their **unique talents** and **gifts** in the light of their individual place and contribution in the body. And this book will help to **mobilize the energies** of the local church into a **Mighty Army** of believers moving and marching to the beat and mandate of the Great Commission. Any healthy **organized** and **functioning** church moving with precision, accuracy and purpose becomes a threat to the enemy and an effective tool in the Hand of the Master.

This is a must read and training tool for pastors, staff, ministry leaders and members who are ready to impact your congregation, community, and city for the cause of Jesus Christ.

Dr. Jimmy R. Stevens

Pastor, New Covenant Faith Baptist Church
President, Lake Charles Bible College

E.J. Kemper III

PREFACE

There are several word pictures used in Holy Scripture to describe God's church. The church is called sheep of the Good Shepherd. The church is pictured as the bride of Christ. The church is also described as a building or a temple of God.

But of all of these word pictures, the body is perhaps the most powerful and the most relatable. Like a body, the church is an organism. Like a body, the church should be organized. Like a body, God expects His church to be functioning. Like a body, God expects His church to be growing. Like a body, the church should be interdependent. Like a body, no one system can support the church. Like a body, the one local church has many members.

In this book, we will look at the seven basic systems of the human body and use them as a model to describe key systems and functions of the local church. Each system represents a critical function in the church. From leadership to evangelism, every area of the church fits into one of theses systems.

It is my belief that by understanding the local church in this light we can better understand the significance of each ministry in the local church.

Furthermore, this model will demonstrate how each member in the body is interrelated and interdependent just as Christ intended. While these systems are distinct in name, role and function they are united in their goal of contributing to a healthy, growing, Christ-exalting church. One system should not be competing with another. One system should not be at odds with another. One system should not be a detriment to another. However, the reality in many local churches is that our ministries are not working together. They are at times at odds with one another. These things should not be!

If we are to be the church that exalts Christ and contributes to the building of His kingdom, we must understand our function as THE LOCAL BODY!

THE SKELETAL SYSTEM
LEADERSHIP

E.J. Kemper III

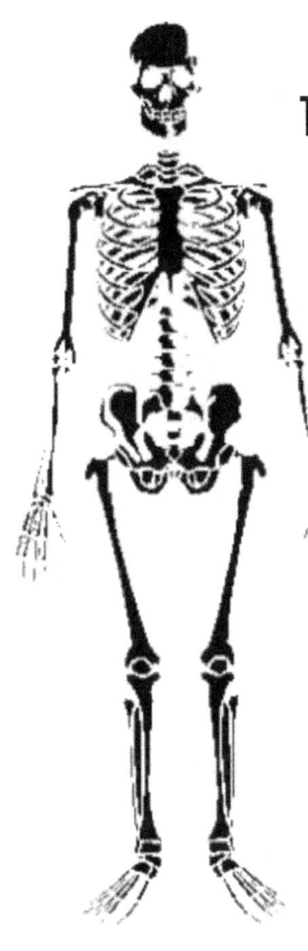

The Skeletal System

Leadership

- Pastoral Staff
- Deacons
- Directors

Functions

- Provides Structure
- Guidance
- Accountability

The skeletal system provides structure for the human body. It is made up of some 206 bones. Along with these are cartilage, tendons, joints, ligaments and connective tissues. All of these components combine to give the human body shape, form, support, protection and mobility.

This is also seen in the local church body. The church body needs structure. This structure is found in the leadership of the local church. This is pastors and associates, deacons and deaconesses, ministry leaders and directors. In John Maxwell's bestseller, The 21

Irrefutable Laws of Leadership, he calls this THE LAW OF THE LID. This means that an organization will go no higher or further than the level of its leadership. Like the skeletal system, leadership in the local body shapes and forms ministry. It supports and mobilizes ministry. Good leadership in the church gives the local body great potential. Good leadership supports the church. Good leadership bears the weight of ministry and gives the church healthy posture. Good leadership in the church consists of multiple leaders who , like the skeletal system, are connected and unified under the vision and mission of the local church. One of the key functions of the skeletal system is protection. Vital organs are protected by the skeletal system.   The brain is protected by the skull. The heart and lungs are protected by the rib cage. Reproductive organs are protected by the pelvic bones. And so too in the local church body.   Strong leadership in the church protects the vital ministries of the church. Like the skeletal system, leadership in the church forms the basis of support that makes most of what the church does possible. Most all of us have used the metaphor that likens leadership to the skeletal system "you've got to have a BACK BONE!" To which I say, "INDEED!"

PROBLEMS IN THIS SYSTEM

However, problems in the skeletal system, like every other system of the body, affects the whole body. Common dysfunctions in the skeletal system are fractures or broken bones, osteoporosis or brittle and fragile bones, arthritis or inflamed joints, and irregular curvatures. All of these dysfunctions in the skeletal system adversely affects the body's ability to function and perform basic movements without assistance and great pain.

All of these dysfunctions can be seen in the leadership of the local church. From fractured and broken leadership to weak and fragile leadership. From inflamed leadership to irregular leadership. And like the human body these dysfunctions adversely affects the churches ability to function and perform its basic mission without great pain. God promised to give every church what it needed to fulfill the mission that He has given us. But far too often critical problems in leadership hinder the church from accomplishing that mission. Broken and fractured leadership immobilizes the local church. Weak and fragile leadership limits the local church. Inflamed leadership disgraces the local church. Irregular leadership mocks the local church.

How many times have we heard or experienced power struggles between members of leadership in the church? How many people do we have in positions in the church who have been far too ineffective for far too long? How many people are leading ministries in the church who don't get along with the very people who they are charged with leading? Far too many churches have people in positions of leadership who care more about the title that they have than they do about the assignment and the people they've been given.

I'm encouraged by what I read in Acts 1:15-26. In these verses the Apostles are obediently waiting in Jerusalem to receive the power of the Holy Spirit that Christ had promised them. During this ten-day waiting period the Apostles pray, worship, gather and fellowship. But in these last verses of chapter one we also find that they raise up Matthias to replace the leadership gap left by Judas. A great application can be made from this action. Before God can use our local churches to have the kind of impact that He desires us to have, we must have good leadership in place!

Pastor Elmore Garner of Mount Calvary Baptist Church in Lake Charles, Louisiana gives us these four nuggets about leadership in the local body. 1. Great leadership must be seasoned by God's Grace! 2. Leadership that loves God will change the world! 3. Poor leadership will never develop new leaders! 4. Bad leadership is like a cancer in the Body of Christ!

The Bible teaches us much about the importance of leadership. Great lessons are learned from studying leaders in the Bible. Strong leaders like Moses, Joshua, David and Samuel give us great examples to follow. Bad leaders like Saul, Ahab, Solomon and others give us examples that we should shun. I encourage you to spend time looking into the leadership of these and many others found in the Bible and write down some of the lessons that might be applied to the local church. The greatest example, however is Jesus. Jesus teaches us that leadership in the local church is about serving. Jesus said "the greatest among you must be servant of all." Think for a moment of Jesus washing His disciples feet and we have the greatest example of what leadership in the local should be about.

WHAT ARE YOUR THOUGHTS?

____

____

____

____

____

____

____

____

____

____

____

____

____

____

The Local Body

E.J. Kemper III

THE MUSCULAR SYSTEM
STEWARDSHIP

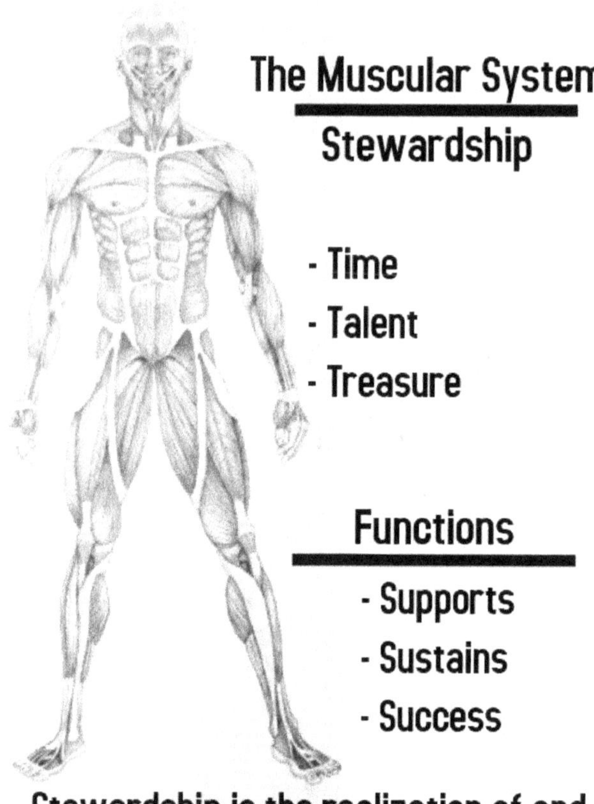

Stewardship is the realization of and response to God's love.

The muscular system is responsible for the movement of the human body. Every action that the human body performs requires the muscular system. From walking to writing, from speaking to breathing, from the beating of the heart to the digesting of food, consciously and unconsciously the muscular system enables the movement of the human body. Think about it, every task that you desire to accomplish is done so with the aid of the muscular system. That's amazing!

Like the muscular system, stewardship in the local church enables its movement. The mission of the church is to reach the lost, disciple the saved, and serve the communities in which they gather. This mission is impossible without the good and faithful stewardship of the members of the local body.

So, what is stewardship? Stewardship is the realization of and response to God's love. Stewardship is the responsible use of all that God has given us. Our stewardship is not only in reference to the church. But God desires every Christian to practice WHOLE LIFE STEWARDSHIP. This is the responsible use of EVERYTHING that He has entrusted to our care. The psalmist declares "the earth is the Lord's and fullness thereof, the world and they that dwell therein." This means that we belong to God. This also means that everything we have belongs to God. God is the creator and sustainer of all things. This also means that we are not owners of our lives but stewards. Therefore, we should exercise wisdom in using that which God has entrusted to us. Stewardship, then, should be over our money, time, health and relationships etc.

In the context of the local church, stewardship is of great importance. If the church is to accomplish the mission that Christ has given us then the members of the local church must give of their time, talent and treasure! If God has given us time and talent (and He has) then certainly a portion of our time and talent should be given to the work of ministry. How many potentially powerful ministries are not able to be sustained because they lack volunteers? How many needed areas of ministry are lacking in the local church because we only want to be ministered to rather than ministering ourselves? God has called every Christian to the work of ministry. It is not merely the responsibility of the pastor and deacons. There is much to be done and our work is never complete. May we all examine the stewardship of our time and talent.

If God has given us treasure (and He has) then certainly a portion of our treasure should be given to the work of ministry. You'd be surprised to know how many members in the local body never give financially to the work of the church. To be clear, God has never asked someone who is poor and without resources to give their last to the church. The myth of the widow's mite needs to be dispelled at once from the church. Christ was not commending the widow who cast her last monies into the treasury of the temple. Nor was Christ, in this instance, using the widow as an example to suggest that Christians give sacrificially. But Jesus highlighted this poor widow casting in her last into the temple treasury as an indictment against the Scribes and Pharisees who "love to go in long clothing, and love salutations in the marketplaces, and the chief seats in the synagogues, and the uppermost rooms at feasts: **which devour widows' houses**, and for a pretense make long prayers: these shall receive greater damnation." Jesus was condemning the practice of that religious system that should have been caring for the poor and the widow but was abusing the poor and the widow.

This aside, far too many abled Christians simply do not give consistently, deliberately and generously to the work of the church. Like any organization the work that the church does comes with economic costs. Therefore, the financial stewardship of the members of the local body enables the church to do all that God has called it to do.

From discipleship to evangelism, from mentoring to small groups, from community outreach to scholarships, stewardship enables the local church to move according to Christ's commission.

PROBLEMS IN THIS SYSTEM

Problems in the muscular system range from simple sprains, strains, spasms and tears to complex diseases and disorders like dystrophy, tendinitis and fibromyalgia. All of these problems in the muscular system limit or stop the entire body's ability to function and perform basic tasks. And so too in the local church. There are the simple problems in stewardship that every church faces. There are certain seasons and months when stewardship wains. Members of the local body should be challenged to consistency in every season of the year. But then there are the complex problems of stewardship. When a church is fulfilling the purpose for which Christ built it then new and unchurched believers will become a part of the local church. These new and unchurched members don't understand the culture of church. They don't speak "Christianese" or understand stewardship lingo. Complex disorders in stewardship develop when the local church fails to disciple and challenge new members to become contributors of their time, talent and treasure. The local church must systematically and intentionally orientate them into the culture of the church.

I want to encourage every member of God's local body to be participating members. Don't leave the great work of the church to the few leaders who are out front. The Bible never makes such a distinction. It makes a distinction in gifts and operations. But the work and expense of ministry should be shared by all the members of the local body. Picture with me the paralyzed man in Mark 2:1-12. This man was able to get to Christ because his four friends each had a corner of his cot and bore that corner faithfully. And so too for each of us, GET YOUR CORNER AND CARRY IT FAITHFULLY!

WHAT ARE YOUR THOUGHTS?

____

____

____

____

____

____

____

____

____

____

E.J. Kemper III

THE DIGESTIVE SYSTEM

DISCIPLESHIP

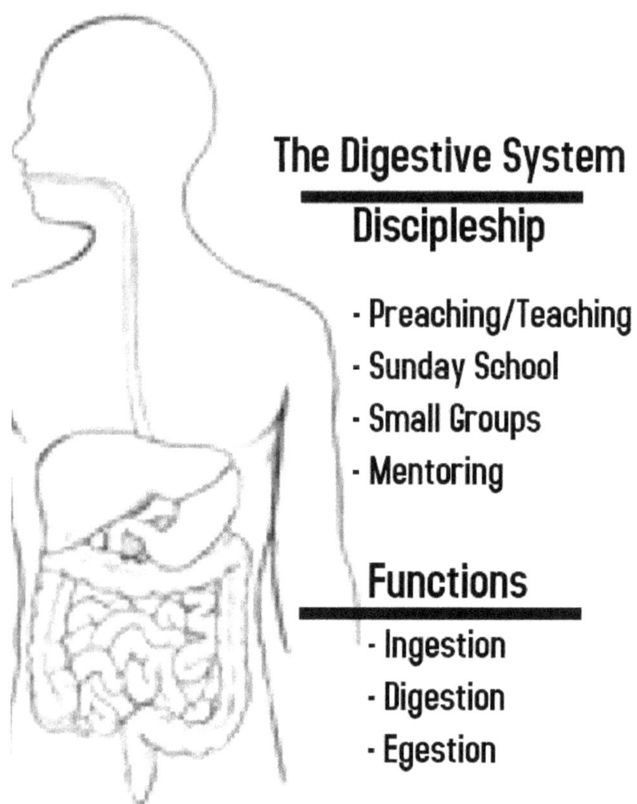

Discipleship is key to individual Christian growth and therefore the key to church growth.

The digestive system is the system of the human body that converts food into basic nutrients and energy to feed the entire body. This is ingestion, digestion and egestion. In order to grow and be healthy, the human body needs food. Good food. Not fast food. But in order for this food to be beneficial to the human body there must be a digestive system. Through a group of organs working together, food is broken down, moistened, swallowed, and absorbed. Nutrients are extracted and waste is excreted. Awesomeness!

Like the human body, the local church needs food in order to grow and be healthy. The local church body needs good food and not fast food. This food is the Word of God. The Bible declares "man shall not live by bread alone but by every Word that proceeds out of the mouth of God". This is the metaphor employed by many authors in the Bible to describe the Word of God. From Ezekiel, David, Isaiah, Paul and even Christ declared the Bible to be SPIRITUAL FOOD.

In order for this spiritual food to be beneficial to the local body there must be DISCIPLESHIP! Discipleship is the process by which the Word of God is broken down chapter by chapter, verse by verse, precept by precept so that it may be understood and applied to the individual Christian life. It is the faithful teaching and preaching of the Word of God that provides the spiritual energy and spiritual nutrition to live a healthy Christian life.

Without food a child's growth is retarded. He or she cannot develop the way God intended if they are not fed a healthy diet. This nutrition is critical to that child. And as children of God, spiritual nutrition is critical to our spiritual health as well. We cannot mature and bear fruit as God intends for every Christian to do if we are not fed a consistent diet of the Word of God. It is for this reason that every Christian must take serious their church membership. We must belong to churches where the whole counsel of the Word is taught. Forgive my forwardness but too many Christians belong to churches for all the wrong reasons. Some have their membership in churches because of the social, political or historical standing of that church. Others have their membership in churches simply because they were raised there and it is "the family's church." When asked of their churches position on matters critical to the Christian faith many of these do not know.

Pastors must have a conviction to preach all of the Bible. It is my conviction that verse-by-verse teaching of the Bible is a critical part of discipleship. Whatever the method to your churches discipleship, there must be present in our churches a systematic way of studying the full counsel of God. We cannot stand on our soapbox or ride our hobby horse. We cannot treat the Word of God like a spiritual buffet where we pick and choose certain parts of Scripture that we seek to know and understand and others that we shun. We cannot accept the parts of Scripture that make us happy and reject the parts that make us uncomfortable. This is how our growth is retarded. All conviction and no encouragement is not the full counsel of God's Word. All health and wealth and no exhortation to holiness is not the full counsel of God's Word. For this reason, discipleship must consist of preaching, teaching, small groups, mentoring, personal study and meditation.

Look again at the digestive system. It is responsible to ingest and digest but it also is responsible for egestion. This is the expelling of waste through urination and excrement. This is so powerful to understand! There is so much in our lives that is not like Christ. When we come to faith in Christ, our sinful proclivities and bad habits do not magically disappear. We are saved by grace through faith in the work of Christ and not by works of our own righteousness. But upon salvation, the Holy Spirit begins His work in our lives. Through the Word of God, the Spirit of God reveals those area of our lives that are not pleasing to God. As we yield to what is revealed through the Word of God and the Spirit's transforming power, we will see areas of our lives that are not pleasing to God expelled from our lives. The old folks would sing "I looked at my hands and they looked new. I looked at my feet and they did too. Things I used to do I just don't do no more and places I used to go I just don't go no more." Hallelujah! This is the work of God through faithful discipleship!

PROBLEMS IN THIS SYSTEM

Problems in the digestive system range from acid reflux to Crohn's disease, from gallstones to irritable bowel syndrome. All of these problems deal with the body's ability to digest food. In the local church, faithful discipleship will encourage, edify, challenge, offend, upset and anger. It also will uncover the proud and stubborn who refuse to accept the truth of God's Word. Some will have trouble digesting some of the hard truths of Scripture. But let us remain faithful and vigilant to the "pulling down of strongholds" through the teaching and preaching of the Word.

Allow me to challenge you now. Advances in technology have afforded the church so many opportunities to do great things for the cause of Christ. Churches are able to broadcast the Gospel through television, radio and internet to places that may not otherwise hear it.   Live-streaming, video hub platforms like YouTube, Vimeo and others allow churches to upload and store years of faithful preaching. Social media platforms also gives churches the power to share Christ through memes and video.   Thank God for these advances.   However, with these great advances come some critical side effects.   Many young (in age and in faith) have abandoned belonging to a local church and have placed their discipleship in the hands of pastors, preachers and teachers that they have found on the internet or on social media. They opt to stay home rather than to congregate. They catch the live-stream rather than showing up in person. This is detrimental to the health of the individual Christian as well as to the health of the local church. Local pastors and teachers can be asked questions and held accountable. Local churches can benefit from the gifts of each individual Christian. And there is nothing like the sharpening experience of gathering with other believers and studying the Word of God together. My friend, do not allow the blessings of technology to replace your church membership. It is a wonderful addition to your membership when used correctly.

WHAT YOU'RE YOUR THOUGHTS

____

____

____

____

____

____

____

____

____

____

____

____

E.J. Kemper III

THE RESPIRATORY SYSTEM
WORSHIP

The Respiratory System

Worship

- Corporate Worship
- Corporate Prayer

Functions

- Inhalation
- Respiration
- Exhalation

Worship causes an upward look to God, an inward look at self and an outward look of obedience.

The human body needs oxygen! Thank God for the respiratory system. The respiratory system is a series of organs responsible for taking in that needed oxygen and expelling carbon dioxide. The primary organs of the respiratory system are the lungs, which carry out this exchange of gases as we breathe. We cannot live without oxygen. It is the fuel of the human body. Deprived of oxygen for only a short time, the human body will die. This is inhalation, respiration and exhalation.

When I think of this I think of worship and prayer. Through worship and prayer we reach up to our God in thanksgiving. Through worship and prayer we cast our cares upon God. Through worship and prayer we consecrate and rededicate ourselves to God. Through worship and prayer our faith and confidence in the Word of God is strengthened. Through worship and prayer we find hope to face the daily challenges of life. Indeed, corporate worship and prayer is a significant part of the local church. Like the respiratory system the worship and prayer life of the local church takes in the refreshing presence of God. It also exhales, expels and exchanges the stale spirit of apathy and indifference. A church deprived of worship and prayer will die. Indeed these are the fuel of the local body.

It is no wonder then that these areas are under attack in the local church. Prayer meetings, altar prayer, consecration and intercessory prayer sound so old school and outdated in the ears of many Christians today. Many churches today can give voice to the "worship wars" and generational gaps that are ever prevalent amongst their members. As I reflect upon the history of the church within the context of the African-American community, I'm reminded of many of the great struggles that we have been through in this country. Worship and prayer has been at the heart of our overcoming and these cannot be abandoned or allowed to be defeated by the enemy.

The stale air of daily struggles should be exhaled every Lord's Day and the fresh, reviving air of hope should be inhaled. This is done through corporate worship and prayer. In corporate worship and prayer, we stand with brothers and sisters of the faith who understand our struggle, worship our God and are seeking Him with us for our good. There is no more beautiful experience in the context of the church that I pastor than that of the saints gathered around the altar, hand in hand, heads bowed and hearts lifted up to God. Have mercy!

Corporate worship and prayer prepare the heart to receive the Word of God! We must endeavor to cease quarrels over genres and styles of music. A church must examine the context of it's congregation and make decisions as to style and genre. I love the old hymns of the church but also understand that not everyone that I pastor feels the same. I cannot be so preoccupied with my own desires that I fail to see the benefit in other forms of music. Let the strong bear the infirmities of the weak!   There are wonderful contemporary CHRIST EXALTING songs that should be welcomed by all generations.   We must make decisions that are best for our context but let's not divide over style and genre.   We miss the true purpose and goal of worship when we simply make it about style and genre.

The local church must call it's members to prayer. Seek God's face. Call on His Name. The Bible declares that prayer is to be made without ceasing.   Furthermore the Bible details the prayer life of Christ. The custom of Christ was to rise early before the start of His day and pray to His Father. Now, if Christ, the Son of God, God Himself, found it necessary to pray, how much more should we? Prayer is not only to be prioritized personally but also corporately.

PROBLEMS IN THIS SYSTEM

Some common problems in the respiratory system are asthma, where air flow becomes restricted; bronchitis, where organs are inflamed due to polluted air being breathed in over a period of time.

Other problems of the respiratory system are influenza, caused by viruses; and laryngitis, caused by an inflamed voice box; and pneumonia, caused by an infection in the lungs. These problems are analogous to those of the local church as it pertains to worship and prayer. We must not allow the flow of worship and prayer to become restricted by outdated traditions. It is often the case that someone brings polluted air to the ministry of music in our churches. If this is left unchecked by leadership it will cause an inflammation in the church and our corporate gatherings will be left coughing, wheezing and gasping for air.

Leaders of music ministry cannot simply be employees of the church. When talent alone is the only criteria for employment then the church opens itself up for viruses. How many local churches have ministers of music who are living openly sinful lives? This sets a standard of hypocrisy and will ultimately hurt the church. Furthermore, we cannot allow one voice in the churches ministry of music to become so puffed up that he or she makes themselves the center of attention and the object of adoration rather than Christ.

It is my prayer that every Sunday the people of God would be refreshed, revived and renewed through the worship and prayer that prepares the heart to receive the Word. It is my prayer that hope and strength would be gained to face the coming challenges of the week. It is my prayer that nothing would restrict the flow of God's Spirit upon the local church each Lord's Day!

WHAT ARE YOU THOUGHTS?

E.J. Kemper III

THE NERVOUS SYSTEM
VISION

E.J. Kemper III

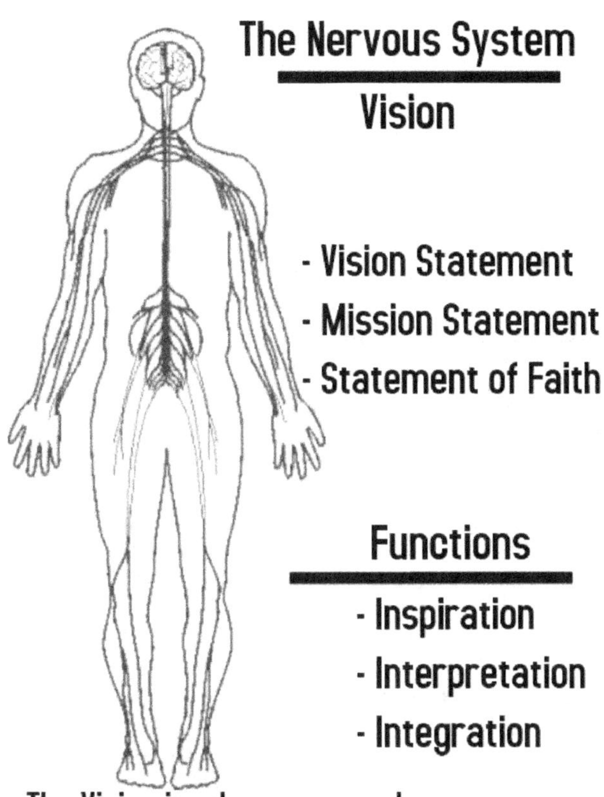

The Vision is who we are, where we are and where we are going.

The nervous system is the part of the human body that sends signals to different parts of the body. It can be understood as the wiring of the body. The nervous system sends and receives messages to and from the brain about what is going on in the body and around the body. This is how the body communicates and reacts to happenings in and around it. The nervous system is made up of the brain, the spinal cord and a large network of nerves throughout the human body. Without the nervous system we cannot know what's going on outside of the body. This is because the nervous system reacts to certain stimuli such as light and weather. Furthermore, without the nervous system the human body has no control over itself. This all happens through sensory and motor nerves. One senses what's happening around the body, the other tells the body how to react to what is sensed.

What the nervous system is to the human body vision is to the local church body. The capitol "V" Vision includes covenants, creeds, statements of faith, mission statements, vision statements and annual themes. The vision of the church sends a signal throughout the whole church. It tells the church who we are, where we are and where we are going. The vision of the church senses what is happening in the church and around the church. The vision of the church mobilizes the church to respond to what has been sensed. Without vision the local church cannot effectively respond to all that is happening in and around it. The vision of the church provides inspiration,   interpretation   and integration.

Every church should know that they are a part of the universal body of Christ and the implications of that. This is where our covenants, creeds and statements of faith come in. It is also important that the local church know what distinguishes it from other churches. This is where the mission and vision statements come in. Every state, city and community is different. Therefore, every church seeking to be relevant and fulfill God's purpose in its context will be different. The vision of the local church must remind, challenge, and inspire the body. It will remind them of who they are distinctly. It will challenge them out of their comfort zone. It will inspire them to see God's purpose in everything they do.

The church must be reminded of its purpose. The ebb and flow of life and ministry oft times causes us to lose sight of why we are doing the things that we are doing. We risk viewing the work of ministry as a chore to be accomplished rather than as a purpose from God to be fulfilled. But when we are reminded of the vision of the church, the mundane is connected to the majestic and pulled from the sinking sand of monotony. The food giveaway is elevated and connected to the words of Christ, "I was hungry and you fed me…" The small groups are elevated and connected to the testimony of Scripture, "and they continued steadfastly in the apostles' doctrine and fellowship, and in breaking of bread, and in prayers…" Even the smallest task is glorified and given greater meaning when understood in light of the vision.

In Matthew 6:22, Jesus declares, "The eye is the lamp of the body. If your vision is clear, your whole body will be full of light." In this verse Jesus tells His listeners to focus upon the things of God. For an analogy He uses the eye and the body. He teaches that if the eye is jumping around from object to object and never focusing on one thing, then the body cannot respond to the things that are most necessary to it. It, like the eye, will be unfocused and unable to connect what is seen to what is being done. In a very real sense, this is what the vision of the local church does for the members of the local church. It helps them to focus on those things most important and encourages them to respond appropriately.

PROBLEMS IN THIS SYSTEM

One disease of the nervous system that we've all heard of is Parkinson's disease. Parkinson's disease happens when there is a problem with certain nerve cells in the brain that control movement. The classic symptoms are shaking, stiff muscles, slow movement, problems with balance, as well as confusion and memory loss. And while it is unclear the cause of this disease of the nervous system, it is clear that the dying of nerve cells is what leads to the loss of muscular control.

Likewise, in the local church body. James, the half-brother of our Lord, teaches that instability comes from being "double minded". Without vision the church moves slow and unsteadily. Without vision the church will be imbalanced. Like Parkinson's disease, a visionless church will gradually get worse. The Biblical book of Judges has a common theme that is repeated within the context of its pages. "And every man did what was right in his own eyes." This is the natural outworking of visionless leadership. Notice Judges begins with the death of a great leader and continues with a subsequent cycle of spiritually sightless leadership. The nation naturally declines into moral decline. This dearth of vision plagues the local church as well.

Vision maintains order, encourages growth and builds upon past successes. Vision produces unity, boosts productivity and creates momentum. Here's an illustration to sum up the power and importance of vision in the local church: *"When Epcot Center was finished in 1982, Walt Disney had already passed away. Disney executives asked Walt's wife to cut the ribbon at the opening ceremony. When she was called up to the podium, one of the executives said to her, "Mrs. Disney, I wish Walt could have seen this." She replied, "He did.""*

Pastor Braylon Harris of Mount Olive Baptist Church of Lake Charles, Louisiana speaks on the importance of vision: "In such a busy, bright and boisterous world vision is vital. There are so many problems and programs, issues and initiatives in which our church can get involved that a clear understanding of what we are called to get involved in is critical to avoiding sensory overload and achieving our overall success. Vision creates a laser like focus on the things that our particular church is uniquely called to, equipped for, and passionate about addressing. While this mitigates sensory overload on one hand it enhances reaction time on the other. There should be things because of our churches clear vision that need minimal explanation to engage maximum participation. Your vision will allow your "yea to be yea" and "your nay to be nay" in the

matters   of   process   and
programming."

WHAT ARE YOUR THOUGHTS?

____

____

____

____

____

____

____

____

____

____

____

____

E.J. Kemper III

THE CIRCULATORY SYSTEM
OUTREACH

The Circulatory System

Outreach

- Community Outreach
- H&H Visitation
- Visitor Contact
- Orientation

Functions

- Share Love
- Meet Needs
- Heal Hurt

Sharing the love of Christ by meeting the needs of our members and aiding in healing the hurt of our communities .

The circulatory system is the system of the human body responsible for circulating blood, oxygen and nutrients throughout the body. The main organ of this system is the heart. The circulatory system is also made up of blood, blood vessels, veins, arteries, capillaries, and cells. The heart pumps blood so that it will travel through vessels to the lungs to exchange carbon dioxide and oxygen. The blood then returns to the heart where it is pumped again throughout the body delivering nutrients, oxygen, and hormones to our cells. The blood then returns back to the heart where this cycle starts all over again.

The circulatory system is analogous of the outreach ministry of the local church. Outreach is how the local church expresses the love of Christ to those not in the local body and those who are suffering within the local body. Hear the oft repeated mantra of the New Testament: BE DOERS OF THE WORD AND NOT HEARERS ONLY! We are called to show the love of Christ by loving our fellow man. Our Savior declared that love is the identifying mark of the Christian. A church that does not love is a contradiction to Christ. A church that does not seek to be a helping presence to the community is a contradiction to Christ. A church that is silent to the issues facing a community is a contradiction to Christ. A church that does not love and care for its own members is a contradiction to Christ.

The goal of hearing the Word of God is that we might live out the Word of God. God has empowered us through the Holy Spirit to practice what we preach. The local church must wisely and intentionally seek ways to be a tangible, visible help in the community that they are situated in. This is not philanthropy! This is ministry! The needs that we meet are not in the name of doing good. They are in the name of Jesus Christ!

The primary mission of Christ and subsequently the local church, was the preaching and teaching of the Word of God. But Christ did not neglect helping those that He came into contact with in the course of preaching and teaching. In fact, helping others was often a great vehicle that Christ used to bring the Word of God to people. And so too for the local church, our good must be done not so as to make sinners comfortable as they go to hell but to make saints out of sinners through the Gospel of Jesus Christ.

PROBLEMS IN THIS SYSTEM

One of the most prevalent problems in the circulatory system is high blood pressure. High blood pressure, also known as hypertension, is when the pressure of the blood being pumped through the arteries is higher than it should be. High blood pressure has been called the "silent killer", because it often has no warning signs or symptoms, and many people do not even know they have it. Over time, the constant pressure overload causes accumulating damage and leads to serious health problems.

Not to get too technical, but I think this is powerful and interesting to note. Blood pressure is set by two things. 1) Cardiac output. The amount of blood pumped by each ventricle in one minute; and 2) Peripheral resistance. The resistance that the heart has to overcome to make the blood flow through the blood vessels of the circulatory system. This basically means that this great problem of high blood pressure is caused by the heart being overworked because of the resistance to its basic function (to cause blood flow). While there are many contributing factors to this, (poor diet, inactivity, heredity, etc) the result is the same. The heart is overworked because of the resistance to the flow of the blood around the body.

This problem of high blood pressure is seen spiritually in the local body as well. DOES THE CHURCH HAVE HIGH BLOOD PRESSURE? The heart of the church is the mind of Christ. The lifeblood of the church is the love of Christ. To each of us the Lord declares "freely you have received, freely you should give." The love of Jesus Christ should circulate through the local church into the community and back again in a continuous cycle. But the question is how much resistance is there in the local church to the "blood flow" throughout the body and community? We must identify those things that are resisting the normal flow of love from the church to the community in which it resides. We will talk about evangelism and global missions in the next chapter. But too many churches seek to help those adversely affected by tragedy and great hardship around the world and never set foot in their own backyard to help those in their local community.

Traditions block the flow of outreach. A theology that views the church like a bank to merely save, invest and grow endlessly bigger blocks the flow of outreach. The church is not a business although there is the business of the church. The church is not a bank though it should seek to use its resources wisely. The church is a ministry! And meeting the needs of those we disciple and wish to gain for Christ is a part of that call. The local church is not a gated community for a few dues-paying members but a neighborhood of the faithful that actively seeks new neighbors to be a part of it.

Pastor Alfred Williams II of New Sunlight Baptist Church in Lake Charles, Louisiana views outreach from this perspective as well. He says, "As blood circulates to give vitality to our bodies, doing outreach enables the church to offer new life and vitality to those struggling with impossible circumstances in the community"

The local church must be challenged with new ideas and relevant strategies to share the love of Christ by sharing the gospel of Christ through the agency of outreach in the name of Christ! The pastor of a once prominent Baptist Church near the city in which I pastor, shares the sad testimony of his church becoming so inwardly focused that they lost sight of what Christ called them to do. This church's building has been put up for sale because the people can no longer afford the multi-building campus. He goes on to share that this campus was built to meet needs and offer assistance in the name of Jesus Christ but somewhere along the line they simply became empty spaces in the way. And his is not the only church to face this sad and fated reality. We must get back to being who we were called to be. The Lord help us!

While so many in the modern church are focusing on "church growth strategies", the simple truth is that we must be outwardly focused if there is to be inward growth. We can have all the bells and whistles and completely fail at what Christ has called us to do. There is a direct correlation between the outward reach of the local church and the inward growth of the local church. We will discuss more on this in the next chapter but I've seen this reality time and again in my experience as a youth pastor and senior pastor. There are seasons when the local church's attention can be so arrested by programs, annual days, and Sunday morning services until we lose sight of outreach. Before you know it months have passed with no tangible effort at reaching out beyond the four walls of the church and into the community. Let us be intentional in our focus on outreach!

WHAT ARE YOUR THOUGHTS?

____
____
____
____
____
____
____
____
____
____

E.J. Kemper III

<u>THE REPRODUCTIVE SYSTEM</u>
EVANGELISM

The Reproductive System

Evangelism

- Personal
- Corporate
- Missions

Functions

- Kingdom Growth
- Church Growth
- Fulfill Purpose

Therefore go and make disciples of all nations, baptizing them in the name of the Father and of the Son and of the Holy Spirit.
- Christ

The reproductive system is that system of the human body responsible for procreation. Like many of the systems already covered, the reproductive system is a collection of internal and external organs that work together to ensure procreation. For that reason, this system is considered one of the most important systems of the human body. This system ensures the existence of humanity.

In order for procreation to be successful there must be the seed (sperm), the womb, the ovulation, the fertilization, the shaping of the fetus, the contractions and the birth!

Have mercy! Can you see the picture of the local church starting to form?

The reproductive system and its processes in the human body can be likened to evangelism in the local church body.   It is through evangelism that spiritual procreation takes place. And the members of the local church MUST work together to ensure this spiritual procreation. God has sovereignly chosen the agency of evangelism through the local church to guarantee the existence of the local church. Just to be clear, the point of evangelism is SPIRITUAL PROCREATION and not numerical duplication. Our motives matter to God and they should matter to us. Our motives should never be to simply put butts in pews. One pastor calls it "the difference between growing and swelling." Growing is the natural outworking of a church fulfilling it's Christ given mandate. Acts chapters 3-6 really shows this. Swelling might look like growth but soon the sickness behind it will be exposed.

So what is evangelism? Evangelism is simply the spreading or communicating of the Christian gospel. There is then a few essential elements of evangelism. There is the content, the context and the conduit of evangelism. The content of evangelism is the gospel of Jesus Christ. That's the meat and potatoes! The word gospel means "good news". And this good news is Jesus Christ. And Jesus Christ is the Son of God, sent to save the world from the inevitable wrath of God the Father by taking that wrath upon Himself at Calvary. We are saved from this wrath by grace through faith in that work of Christ on Calvary. That is the content of evangelism.

This is where the blurred lines and confusion about evangelism comes in. The context and the conduit. For many, the word evangelism evokes a particular picture. Perhaps there's the thought of a group of people knocking on a door with a Bible and a prepared script. For others the thought of a pastor standing on a street corner holding a sign and a bullhorn shouting "repent and be saved!", comes to mind.

Let me quickly dispel this myth! The context of evangelism is the terrain of everyday life BECAUSE THE CONDUIT OF EVANGELISM IS EVERYDAY CHRISTIANS! **(Tweet that, Facebook that, Instagram that, Snapchat that)** The context of evangelism is the terrain of everyday life because the conduit of evangelism is everyday Christians. This means that evangelism is not only the responsibility of the pastor and deacons. The call to be a witness is for every Christian. The time and place for us to be witnesses is everyday and at all times. This means that the local church should have scheduled time for evangelism. The local church should challenge the body to corporate evangelism and missions. But the most effective evangelistic method is through the Christian's personal relationships. There are folk who don't know Christ but know us. And because they know us, their chances of coming to know Christ should be greater. This is powerful to the church to grasp. God sovereignly uses the personality, language, expressions and stage of each Christian as a tool to reach out to those who are not saved. The content of evangelism is the gospel. The context of evangelism is everyday life. The conduit of evangelism is every Christian.

Like the reproductive system of the human body, evangelism in the local body ensures the existence of that local body. The gospel is the seed. The world is the womb. And every unsaved person is like an unfertilized egg needing only the seed of the gospel to become an embryo. Note another sobering comparison between the reproductive system and evangelism: NOT EVERY EGG IS FERTILIZED WHEN IT COMES IN CONTACT WITH THE SEED. Every person that hears the gospel will not become a Christian. Some will reject the gospel. Some will keep it in their hearts until another time. But the local church and each member of that local church are responsible for sharing the seed of the gospel.

PROBLEMS IN THIS SYSTEM

If the purpose of the reproductive system is to procreate then the problem of this system (for the purposes of this work) is infertility. This is a couples inability to reproduce after at least one year of trying. There are many causes of infertility. There is low sperm cell count, no sperm cell count, hormone disorders, cancers and blockages in the reproductive organs. An interesting truth that arrested my attention was the infertility caused by STD's (sexually transmitted diseases). These are infections that cause low sperm cells and other reproductive disorders that prevent procreation. In the event of pregnancy and birth, STD's cause many after birth complications.

Perhaps this can be seen in the local church as well. **DOES THE LOCAL CHURCH HAVE A STD? Sinfully Transmitted Diseases?!?!** When the local church is more focused on saints being happy then sinners being saved, it has a sinfully transmitted disease. When the focus of our outreach is mere philanthropy rather than the gospel of Christ, it has a sinfully transmitted disease. When our members show up by the hundreds to business meeting but only by the tens to the tent meeting, it has a sinfully transmitted disease.

We must remember that the goal of evangelism is not to merely see the unsaved saved but to see them discipled into being committed followers of Christ. And so these sinfully transmitted diseases can affect even the new Christian's journey to being a committed follower of Christ.

Dr. Samuel Tolbert, pastor of Greater St. Mary Missionary Baptist Church and President of the National Baptist Convention of America, shared with me on the importance of evangelism and mission in the local church. "Evangelism and Mission are both essential biblical assignments of God's church. Our God of love has chosen to express His love through the church utilizing evangelism and mission. God is focused on the salvation of souls and the social well-being of people. Evangelism is the loving delivery of the Gospel to the unregenerate utilizing multiple and relevant paradigms. Mission is meeting the social and physical needs of humanity that works to prepare the hearts of people to be receptive for the Gospel of Jesus Christ. The believer has been issued a commandment to engage in evangelism and mission."

WHAT ARE YOUR THOUGHTS?

E.J. Kemper III

<u>FINAL THOUGHTS</u>

WHERE WE GO FROM HERE

Jesus declared "on this rock I will build my church and the gates of hell will not prevail against it." This declaration and promise of Christ gives us hope in the midst of everything that comes against the church. However, this promise is of God's universal church. The inevitability of each of our local churches are not given such a promise. The doors of local churches are closing every day. Statistics show this to be an alarming trend. Gifted pastors and leaders are leaving local churches every month.

God has given the local church everything that it needs to stem this tide of defections. But we have to get serious about the issues that have lingered in churches for far too long. We have to get serious about the generational gaps and worship wars. We have to get serious about leadership struggles and false doctrine. We have to get serious about new and traditional methods of ministry. The local church cannot afford to allow these and other issues to go unchecked for another generation.

The great hope that I find is that there are local churches all over this nation that are getting it right. Churches that are not afraid of new ideas. Churches that honor the old but welcome the new. Churches that are theologically sound and socially engaged. It's not enough to be theologically right if you are socially wrong. And it's not enough to be socially right if you are theologically wrong.

The hope of this work is to challenge the local church to renewed focus on the great labor that Christ has called us to. The seven basic systems of the human body are distinct in their functions yet interdependent and united in their goal of being a healthy body. When a problem arises in any of these systems it affects the whole.

E.J. Kemper III

Osteoporosis is not merely a problem for the skeletal system, it's a problem for the body. Spasms and strains are not merely problems for the muscular system, they are problems for the body. And so on.

And so too in the local body. Each ministry in the local church is distinct in its function but it must also be interdependent and united in the goal of being a healthy church. It is my prayer that this picture of the local church has been a great encouragement to everyone that reads it.

The Lord bless you!

EJ Kemper III was born to a teacher and a preacher in Fort Polk, Louisiana. He is a veteran of the U.S. Army, a graduate of GMOR Theological Institute and pastor of Mount Pilgrim Baptist Church in Lake Charles, LA. EJ has traveled as a missionary, sat on the board of charitable organizations, written numerous columns in Christian magazines and authored six books.

Pastor Kemper is the husband of Orelia Marie Kemper and the father of Ellis James Kemper IV and Eyana Janae Kemper.

www.ingramcontent.com/pod-product-compliance
Lightning Source LLC
Chambersburg PA
CBHW061817250726
48657CB00001B/465